Clifton Park - Halfmoon Public Library

BOOK WORMS

Earth Matters
Oceans

Dana Meachen Rau

7504

mc **Marshall Cavendish**
Benchmark
New York

2

Jump over the waves. Swim in the salty water. Sail in a boat. It is fun to play in the ocean.

Oceans cover planet Earth. In fact, more of Earth's surface is ocean than land. Oceans cover about two-thirds of Earth.

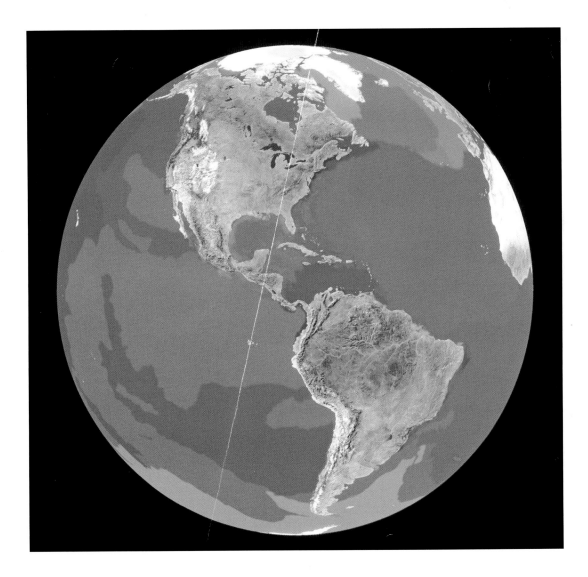

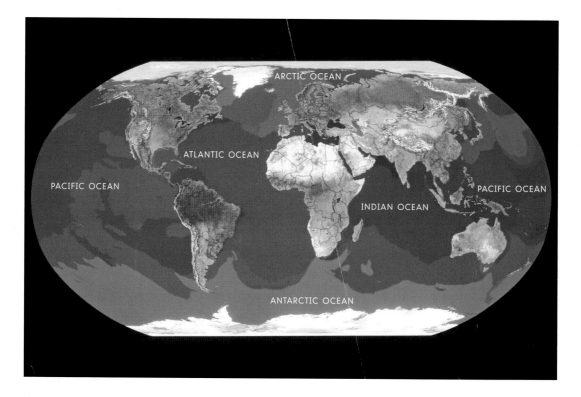

The main oceans are the Pacific, Atlantic, Indian, Arctic, and Antarctic. The Pacific Ocean is much larger than the others. All of the oceans are connected.

The *coast* is where land
meets the ocean.

The water is not deep near the coast. It is *shallow*. But in some places, the ocean is very deep.

The bottom of the ocean is called the ocean floor. The ocean floor is not flat. Its deepest areas are called *trenches*.

The ocean also has underwater mountains. Some mountains poke above the surface. Then they are *islands*.

Sunlight shines into the top of the ocean. This is where most fish live and plants grow.

The deeper you go in the ocean, the darker it gets.

There is also more *pressure* in the deep ocean. Pressure is the weight of the water above you.

17

Oceanographers dive deep to learn more about the ocean. They use strong ships called *submarines* that cannot be crushed by the pressure. Submarines also have bright lights to see in the dark.

Water in the ocean does not stay still. Wind makes *waves* on the surface of the water. It pushes these waves toward the coast. The waves break on the shore.

22

Currents are made by wind, too. Currents are paths of fast-moving water in the ocean. The Gulf Stream is a current that circles around the Atlantic.

Tides are the rise and fall of the ocean's surface. At high tide, water comes high on the beach. Boats can get close to the shore.

At low tide, water goes out from the shore. You can look for crabs in the sand.

People use the ocean. They fish for food. They drill for oil under the ocean floor.

Ships cross the ocean to bring people from one place to another.

Challenge Words

coast (kohst)—Where land meets the ocean.

currents (KUR-ehnts)—Paths of fast-moving water in the ocean.

islands (EYE-lands)—Land surrounded by water on all sides.

oceanographers (oh-sheh-NAH-grah-fehrs)—People who study the ocean.

pressure (PRESH-ehr)—The weight of water.

shallow (SHAL-oh)—Not deep.

submarines (SUB-mar-eenz)—Strong ships that can dive deep in the ocean.

tides—The rise and fall of the ocean's surface.

trenches—Deep areas underwater.

waves—Ripples on the surface of the ocean that move through the water.

Index

Page numbers in **boldface** are illustrations.

With thanks to Nanci Vargus, Ed.D., and Beth Walker Gambro, reading consultants

Marshall Cavendish Benchmark
99 White Plains Road
Tarrytown, New York 10591-5502
www.marshallcavendish.us

Library of Congress Cataloging-in-Publication Data

Rau, Dana Meachen, 1971–
Oceans / by Dana Meachen Rau.
p. cm. — (Bookworms. Earth matters)
Summary: "Discusses the role of the oceans on Earth and introduces waves, tides, and water pressure"—Provided by publisher.
Includes index.
ISBN 978-0-7614-3048-3
1. Ocean—Juvenile literature. I. Title.
GC21.5.R38 2008
551.46—dc22
2007030281

Editor: Christina Gardeski
Publisher: Michelle Bisson
Designer: Virginia Pope
Art Director: Anahid Hamparian

Photo Research by Anne Burns Images

Cover Photo by *Photo Researchers*/F. Stuart Westmorland

The photographs in this book are used with permission and through the courtesy of:
Photo Researchers: p. 1 William Ervin; p. 8 Jeffrey Greenberg; p. 14 Gregory Ochocki; p. 15 B.Murton/Southampton Oceanography Centre; p. 11 Alexis Rosenfeld; p. 17 Dr. Ken MacDonald; p. 21 William Ervin. *Corbis*: p. 2 John Henley; pp. 5, 6 Tom Van Sant; p. 9 Larry Dale; p. 18 Ralph White; p. 22 NASA; p. 26 Ecoscene/Richard Glover. *Peter Arnold*: p. 12 Franco Banfi; p. 29 Jim Wark. *Alamy Images*: p. 25 IML Image Group.

Printed in Malaysia
1 3 5 6 4 2